TOP 20 STARTUP IDEAS TO WATCH IN 2024 - 2026

Stephan S. Sunn

Davidson Global & Co.

Copyright © 2024 Stephan S. Sunn

©Copyright 2024 -2027 Stephan S. Sunn All Rights Reserved

Disclaimer:

This book may not be reproduced or transmitted in any form without the written permission of the authors. Every effort has been made to make this guide as complete and accurate as possible. Although the authors have prepared this guide with the greatest of care, and have made every effort to ensure its accuracy, we assume no responsibility or liability for errors, inaccuracies, or omissions. Before you begin, check with the appropriate authorities to ensure compliance with all laws and regulations. Every effort has been made to make this report as complete and accurate as possible. However, there may be mistakes in typography or content. Also, this report contains information on online marketing and technology only up to the publishing date. Therefore, this report should be used as a guide – not as the ultimate source of Internet marketing information. The purpose of this report is to educate. The authors do not warrant that the information contained in this report is fully complete and shall not be responsible for any errors or omissions. The authors shall have neither liability nor responsibility to any person or entity concerning any loss or damage caused or alleged to be caused directly or indirectly by this report, nor do we make any claims or promises of our ability to generate income by using any of this information.

Davidsons Global & Co. LLC, Davidson, NC 28036, USA; All Inquiries of copyrights, and cooperation go to: Stephan.sunn@aya.yale.edu

CONTENTS

Title Page
Copyright
Preface
Chapter 1: New Era of Startups
Chapter 2: AI-Powered Healthcare Solutions
Chapter 3: Climate Tech and Sustainability
Chapter 4: Future of Work Technologies
Chapter 5: Fintech 2.0
Chapter 6: Smart City Technologies
Chapter 7: Evolution in Education Technology
Chapter 8: Agriculture and Food Technology
Chapter 9: New IoT and Smart Manufacturing
Chapter 10: New Consumer Technology
Chapter 11: Virtual Reality & Augmented Reality
Chapter 12: Autonomous & Intelligent Transportation
Chapter 13: Blockchain and Web3 Startups
Chapter 14: Deep Tech Opportunities
Chapter 15: Building a Future-Proof Startup
Acknowledgement
About The Author
Books By This Author

PREFACE

In a world of change at warp speed, entrepreneurial ventures will better leverage the landscape to create transformational change in industries. This book focuses on twenty technology sectors where innovation is urgent and rewarding, ranging from AI-driven healthcare to climate tech, among others. We believe these areas offer fertile ground for entrepreneurs to create solutions that address pressing global challenges while delivering measurable value. In fact, these industries represent some of the finest opportunities for investors to realize potentially accelerated capital growth and returns, while at the same time enabling business enterprises to meet the ever-evolving demands of the marketplace.

Our approach in this book is not to prescribe a definitive list of the industries that one must pursue but rather to provide a structured guide for aspiring founders. We have highlighted those sectors as opportunities based on the demand witnessed by our clients and partners, who seek innovative tools to be competitive and agile since landscapes continuously shift. We show pathways, insights, and strategies that one should consider in making navigational choices on which one to enter.

Whereas this volume focuses on strategic market entry and industry selection, future volumes will delve into other key elements: how to raise funding, how to develop robust teams, and how to create that kind of visionary entrepreneurial mindset that can turn a person's vision into reality. Our goal is to inspire, but also provide you with the solid foundation needed to start building impactful and capital-ready startups.

CHAPTER 1: NEW ERA OF STARTUPS

The entrepreneurial scene of 2024-2026 stands at a juncture where technological advancement, societal transformation, and economic realignment introduce a turning point. This new era of entrepreneurship is defined by unparalleled opportunities arising out of global shifts in the way we work, live, and do business. Here, we discuss a few major trends that form a significant backdrop through which entrepreneurs build successful ventures in this dynamic world of changing times.

Global Macrotrends Reshaping Startups

Business Model Transformations in the Post-Pandemic Era

The global pandemic accelerated the digital transformation process across industries by nearly a decade, proving to be a strong catalyst for business model innovation. This has set in motion a new normal where hybrid operations are considered default and the going digital-first is no longer an option but an imperative. Successful startups latch onto these newly transformed expectations to create solutions that will seamlessly blend physical and digital experiences while prioritizing resilience and adaptability.

Traditional industry boundaries are increasingly irrelevant, and the most successful recent startups have thrived at the intersection of multiple industries. Health providers seamlessly mix today with fitness technologies, as academic institutions work in close collaboration with professional learning services. This trend makes new business models - which can 'capture' value across previously separate domains - far more viable.

Geopolitical Shifts Affecting Global Market Access

The rebalancing of global supply chains and trade relationships has come with the opportunity for startups to fill critical gaps in the world of international business. Regional trade agreements, along with shifting diplomatic relationships, have granted access to new markets while enabling new challenges that only innovative startups can solve.

If entrepreneurs today have to work through a world of international regulations and various requirements for market access, that nightmare itself ensures opportunities for startups whose solutions make cross-border operations seamless. From supply chain optimization to regulatory compliance platforms, successful ventures are rising to meet these new market needs.

The Rise of Remote-First Business Cultures

But today, this mainstream adoption has turned into something other than a mere temporary measure for containing the infection. It has, in fact, become strategic leverage for organizations. And opens up huge opportunities for startups working on virtual collaboration and team cohesion, digital workplace culture development, cross-cultural communication tools, asynchronous productivity optimization, and remote team wellness and engagement, such as

- Virtual collaboration and team cohesion
- Digital workplace culture development
- Cross-cultural communication tools
- Asynchronous productivity optimization
- Remote team wellness and engagement

In fact, successful founders are building solutions that address not only the technical aspects but also the human elements of remote work: managing distributed teams and aligning cultures.

Emerging Funding Landscapes

Evolution of Venture Capital in Different Regions

We can see how venture capital is becoming regionally diverse, with a wide array of investment trends in the various global markets. While Silicon Valley remains quite influential, there is a new startup landscape blooming in areas such as:

- Southeast Asia, driven by rapid digital adoption, along with an increasingly tech-savvy demographic base;
- Latin America, once the perpetual lender of last resort for local economies during weak currency turmoil, is currently receiving unprecedented investment driven by fintech and e-commerce innovations;
- Africa, from mobile-first products to targeting critical infrastructure shortfalls;
- Eastern Europe, with its rich tradition of deep tech skills creates a compelling value proposition.

Of course, each region carries its unique challenges and opportunities; accordingly, entrepreneurs must alter their financing strategies.

New Financing Models

Traditional venture capital is being supplemented with innovative financing structures to allow flexibility for entrepreneurs and better alignment with their business models. Revenue-based financing, in particular, has gained prominence for startups with predictable recurring revenue streams. The model also provides founders with the opportunity to retain more equity ownership, while investors can have secured returns.

Asset tokenization and blockchain-based financing mechanisms allow for new ways of fundraising and participation by investors.

The new models allow:

- Fractional asset ownership
- Increased liquidity for traditionally illiquid investments
- Wider participation of investors from beyond geographical boundaries
- More transparent and efficient mechanisms of capital allocation

Region-specific Investment Preferences

In the journey to raise capital, understanding regional investment preferences is becoming critical. If North American investors focus on scalability and market size, European investors use sustainability and social impact more often. Practical applications with a clear path to profitability are common in the Asian markets.

These regional differences will further percolate into:

- Expected growth trajectories
- Profit margin expectations
- Choice of timeline for exit
- Governance structure
- Social and environmental impact considerations

The successful entrepreneur hence develops the storyline of his pitch or the business model, keeping in mind the local preference, but also making sure that it makes sense if taken on a global platform.

Way Ahead

The entrepreneurial ecosystem between 2024 and 2026 promises tremendous opportunities amidst overwhelming challenges. The same set of challenges provides the key to success, wherein the entrepreneur must:

- Develop solutions relevant to the globe with sensitivity to the needs of the local market
- Leverage technology to optimum use without losing sight of human needs

- Stay agile through the process of navigating complex regulatory environments
- Design business models that become sustainable within a context of rapid change;
- Develop funding strategies linked with regional market dynamics.

Only those startups can survive in this era that merges technological innovation with cultural sensitivity, respect for regulations, and business sustainability. This will give the basic understanding through which successful ventures should be built in this new era of entrepreneurship as we explore the specific opportunities across different sectors in the following chapters.

CHAPTER 2: AI-POWERED HEALTHCARE SOLUTIONS

Artificial Intelligence and healthcare represent arguably one of the most promising entrepreneurial frontiers yet. As healthcare systems all over the world struggle to meet growing demands, encounter aging populations, and face resource constraints, AI-powered solutions are fast emerging as critical tools in pursuit of better healthcare delivery, access, and improved outcomes.

Predictive Analytics for the Prevention of Health Conditions

Integration with Wearables and IoT Devices

The new era of wearable devices and IoT sensors has exploded onto the scene, creating unparalleled opportunities for continuous health monitoring and early intervention. Successful startups in this space build sophisticated, multilayered platforms that aggregate and analyze real-time health data from multiple sources, use machine learning algorithms to create personalized health insights, render actionable recommendations for lifestyle modification, enable early detection of potential issues in health, and facilitate seamless communication between the patient and healthcare provider.

Success consists of the development of algorithms that will process volumes of sensor data with large throughput; this must be done in a manner that maintains high levels of accuracy and clinical relevance.

Successful platforms need to address issues related to privacy and other regulatory compliances, each governed by its own set of laws and guidelines.

Personalized Health Risk Assessment Systems

Advanced AI algorithms around individual health risk assessment are finding their place in mainstream applications. Entrepreneurs are creating intelligent platforms designed to:
- Determine genetic predispositions associated with a pattern of lifestyle factors
- Consider environmental influences on health outcomes
- Include familial medical history and demographic information, as well as health trends within specific local populations and their risk factors
- Develop prevention plans that are personalized

This type of system is particularly crucial for healthcare providers and insurance carriers needing to optimize resource use and trigger interventions with a proactive interest in preventive medicine.

Mental Health Tech Innovations

AI-powered Therapy Assistance Platforms

The accelerating mental health crisis around the world contributes to faster development and time-to-market for AI-powered mental health solutions. Successful start-ups will focus on:
- Natural language processing for emotion detection and analysis
- Automated cognitive behavioral therapy modules
- Personalized intervention recommendations
- Crisis prediction and prevention systems
- Integration with traditional mental healthcare delivery

The best models are those that hybridize AI capabilities with human oversight to maximize accessibility with quality of care.

Corporate Mental Wellness Solutions

There are great opportunities in the workplace mental health market with innovative solutions that help monitor and analyze stress indicators at the workplace, with early warning systems for burnout:
- Monitor and analyze workplace stress indicators
- Provide early warning systems for burnout
- Facilitate anonymous mental health support
- Track and improve team psychological safety
- Measure the impact of wellness initiatives on productivity

The successful entrepreneurs selling into this space know how to balance the need for employee privacy with organizational insight, demonstrating very clear ROI via improved employee retention and productivity metrics.

Healthcare Data Interoperability Solutions

Cross-border Medical Data Exchange Platforms

Fragmentation in healthcare data across systems and jurisdictions provides an enormous opportunity for startups focused on:
- Secure international health record transfer
- Processing multi-language medical documentation
- Standards-based data transformation
- Real-time health information exchange
- Emergency access protocols for critical care situations

The successful platform needs to deal with the complex regulatory landscape while ensuring the highest levels of data security and patient privacy.

Privacy-Preserving Health Data Marketplaces

As the value of healthcare data increases, so do the opportunities for platforms that enable sharing that data securely and in ways that protect the individual's privacy. Key features include:

- Federated learning implementations to enable distributed data analysis
- Blockchain-based audit trails for data access
- Smart contracts for automated data-sharing agreements
- Tokenization systems to allow monetization of data
- Analytics that preserve privacy

Market Entry Strategies and Success Factors

Regulatory Navigation

Successful healthcare AI startups need to develop multi-layered approaches toward:

- Obtaining relevant certifications - FDA, CE, etc.
- Ensuring compliance with HIPAA, GDPR, and other regional regulations
- Addressing requirements related to clinical validation
- Maintaining the due documentation for regulatory audits
- Being agile within consistently updated regulatory frameworks

Building Trust and Credibility

Healthcare interventions need unparalleled trust-building and trust-sustaining via:
- Transparent AI decision-making
- Transparent articulation of limitations and capabilities
- Periodic performance validation of algorithms
- Close relationships with healthcare institutions
- Ongoing engagement with clinicians

Scaling Considerations

Successful scaling in healthcare AI requires a watchful eye on:
- Quality and diverse populations
- Cultural considerations related to healthcare delivery
- Local medical practices
- Infrastructure capabilities across target markets
- Integration needs of local healthcare systems

Future Outlook

The future of AI-powered healthcare solutions offers immense opportunities to entrepreneurs who can effectively:
- Develop solutions to fit seamlessly within today's healthcare workflows
- Build robust, scalable platforms with high accuracy across diverse populations
- Navigate complex regulatory environments while sustaining innovation velocity
- Build trust on behalf of healthcare providers and patients
- Clearly articulate clinical and economic value propositions

As healthcare systems continue to evolve worldwide, so will the demand for AI-powered solutions. Successful entrepreneurs in this space will be those who can merge technical innovation with deep knowledge of healthcare delivery challenges while keeping the focus on patient safety and data security.

While AI-powered healthcare offers enormous opportunities, tapping them would require due attention to varied regulatory requirements, clinical validation, and stakeholder engagement. Entrepreneurial teams that can help address these challenges, while bringing effective improvement to healthcare outcomes, will find significant avenues of growth and impact in this critical sector.

CHAPTER 3: CLIMATE TECH AND SUSTAINABILITY

As the world shifts to center more efforts on combating climate change, the climate technology and sustainability industry offers unparalleled opportunities for entrepreneurial innovation. With governments across the world tightening environmental policies and companies promising net-zero promises, startups offering practical solutions to environmental challenges are standing tall.

Carbon Capture and Trading Platforms

SME-focused Carbon Credit Marketplaces

Democratization of carbon markets is a huge opportunity that calls for entrepreneurial innovation. Large corporations previously dominated carbon trading, though the SMEs are increasingly looking forward to participating in the market. Successful startups develop platforms that will:

- Simplify carbon credit verification processes
- Offer accessible carbon accounting tools
- Allow fractional carbon credit trading
- Allow peer-to-peer carbon offset transactions to be facilitated
- Automate compliance reporting

These platforms have to strike a balance between being all-inclusive and setting high verification standards so that market integrity is not compromised in the process of opening up participation bases.

Supply Chain Emission Tracking Systems

The fact that modern supply chains are intricate presents substantial opportunities for startups dealing in emissions tracking and reduction. Some of the hallmark features of such platforms include:

- Real-time monitoring of emissions across tiers in the supply chain
- Automatic data gathering from disparate sources

- Standardized methods of calculating emissions
- Performance benchmarking of suppliers
- Suggestions for optimization for reduction

Entrepreneurs in this space must address the challenges of data standardization while providing actionable insights for supply chain optimization.

Circular Economy Enablers

Waste-to-Resource Marketplaces

The increasing momentum of circular economy models is giving way to new opportunities in platforms that make possible the reuse of materials considered waste. The startups that have succeeded so far do this by:

- Matching waste generators with potential users
- Ensuring the quality and composition of materials
- Allowing safe transactions to take place
- Ensuring regulatory compliance
- Tracking environmental impact metrics

These platforms also struggle with logistical issues when they have to build more liquid markets for what had been a previously undervalued material.

Remanufacturing Optimization Platforms

Growth in remanufacturing creates opportunities for startups that have developed technologies to:

- Test the recoverability of a product
- Optimize disassembly processes
- Track lifecycle data on the component
- Manage reverse logistics
- Calculate remanufacturing ROI

Success within this sector requires deep knowledge of manufacturing processes and an in-depth understanding of the operating principles of the circular economy.

Climate Fintech Solutions

Green Investment Platforms

The growth in demand for sustainable investments unleashes innovation at the frontier of finance. Successful platforms:

- ESG-focused investment products
- Impact investment tracking
- Green project funding mechanisms
- Sustainable portfolio optimization
- Real-time impact reporting

Entrepreneurs have to navigate through the complexities of financial regulation without losing transparency in impact measurement.

Environmental Impact Scoring Systems

The need for standardized environmental impact assessment creates opportunities for startups working on developing:

- Automated ESG scoring mechanisms
- Real-time monitoring of environmental performance
- Industry-specific benchmarking
- Predictive analytics of environmental risk
- Standardized impact reporting frameworks

Market Development Strategies

Building Market Trust

Climate tech success depends upon the establishment of credibility grounded on the following aspects:

- Partnerships based on third-party verification
- Transparent documentation of methodology
- Regular audits of impact
- Scientific advisory boards • Industry association engagement

Regional Adaptation

Climate solutions need to be adapted for regional contexts, considering:

- Local regulatory frameworks
- Market maturity levels
- Infrastructure capabilities

- Cultural attitudes toward sustainability
- Economic development priorities

Technology Integration Successful platforms tap into multiple technologies:

• IoT sensors for data collection • Blockchain for transparency • AI for optimization • Cloud computing for scalability • Mobile solutions for accessibility

Success Factors

Regulatory Navigation

Climate tech startups have to adequately navigate:

- Carbon market regulations
- Environmental Compliance
- Cross-border transaction rules
- Data privacy standards
- Industry-specific regulations

Impact Measurement

Successful ventures show their impact through:

- Quantifiable emissions reduction
- Resource conservation metrics
- Calculation of economic benefit
- Social impact assessment
- Indicators of long-term sustainability

Scaling Strategy

To scale effectively, one needs to focus on:

- Market education needs
- Partnership development
- Technology infrastructure
- Operational efficiency
- Customer acquisition costs

Future Outlook

The climate tech sector opens up large opportunities for entrepreneurs who can provide scalable solutions that have the ability to address urgent environmental needs while clearly explaining the value proposition both from an environmental and economic perspective, with an ability to navigate complex regula story systems and innovate simultaneously. They need to build trust through transparent ways of impact measurements and adapt solutions for regional diversity.

As the need for people to act concerning global warming becomes stronger, the demand for innovative climate solutions will only continue to mount. The entrepreneurs who will manage to become successful will be those who can:

- Identify particular market gaps in the sustainability ecosystem
- Design practical solutions that ensure the measurable impact is achieved
- Create sustainable business models that align environmental and economic benefits
- Build robust partnerships with other players across the climate tech ecosystem
- Keep flexibility in adapting to evolving regulatory requirements

The opportunities in climate tech come with immense environmental impact but hold significant economic potential. Entrepreneurs who can put together technological innovation with practical strategies for implementation, while maintaining rigorous impact measurement, will find ample opportunities for growth and impact in this critical sector.

Success here means being very attentive to market dynamics, stakeholder needs, and regulatory requirements, all while maintaining a strong commitment to environmental impact. As this sector evolves further, those entrepreneurs who will shine through such challenges by delivering on the promise of measurable sustainability improvements will emerge successful in the end.

CHAPTER 4: FUTURE OF WORK TECHNOLOGIES

The evolution of the way work is conducted and where it is completed is one of the most fundamental changes in modern business. With organizations across the world adapting to new hybrid models of working and with expectations from the workforce changing, entrepreneurs have never had a better opportunity to shape the way work is conceived by using cutting-edge technologies.

Remote Work Optimization Platforms

Cross-cultural Collaboration Tools

In other words, the globalization of talent brought an immediate need for platforms that enable effective cross-cultural collaboration. Successful startups in this space develop solutions to provide

- real-time cultural context awareness,
- multilingual communication,
- time zone-optimized scheduling,
- diverse communication style support,
- monitoring and improvement of team inclusion metrics.

The platforms would have to balance technological sophistication with practical usability and sensitivity to cultural nuances.

Asynchronous Workflow Solutions

This shift to distributed teams has created an exponential demand for effectively managing asynchronous work. The hallmarks of successful platforms include:

- Intelligent work documentation systems
- Knowledge capture and sharing automation
- Context-rich communication tools
- Progress tracking and visibility

- Smart notification management

But here lies the main challenge for the entrepreneurs: to keep the team cohesive and productive while supporting flexible working arrangements.

Skills-based Talent Marketplaces

AI-powered Skill Verification Systems

The future of work requires a more sophisticated approach to competence assessment and validation. New platforms emerge now that include:

- An analysis of real work produced in the world
- Adaptive skill assessments
- Tracking of skills development over time
- Issuance of validated skill credentials
- Matching of skills with emerging job requirements

Success here calls for sophisticated algorithms with the right assessment of both technical and soft skills.

Global Talent Pooling Platforms

Democratization of work opportunities is driving innovation in talent pooling solutions that:

- Enable borderless team formation
- Compliant global hiring
- Cross-border payments management
- Cultural integration support
- Flexible engagement models

These platforms need to respond to significant international employment legislation challenges without disrupting seamless experiences for employers and talent.

Workplace Wellness Technology

Digital Ergonomics Solutions

The exceptionally high momentum of remote work has caused traction in digital solutions focused on:

- Artificial Intelligence-powered posture analysis
- Workspace optimization suggestions
- Environmental wellness monitoring
- Activity pattern analysis
- Personalized ergonomic guidance

Successful solutions combine hardware and software elements to provide holistic wellness environments.

Team Cohesion Analytics

Team dynamics understanding and maintenance in distributed environments require innovative approaches to communication pattern analysis, collaboration effectiveness measurement, continuous team sentiment monitoring, virtual team building facilitation, and engagement optimization.

Market Implementation Strategies

Enterprise Integration

Any enterprise workplace technology solution has to keep in mind the following aspects:

- compatibility with legacy systems,
- security and compliance requirements,
- scalability across large departments,
- patterns in user adoption,
- ROI measurement frameworks.

Privacy and Ethics

Workplace monitoring in general needs to maintain boundaries on the following fronts:

- data collection policies,
- consent management for employees,
- transparency in analytics practices,
- ethical AI implementation,
- regular auditing of privacy.

Global Deployment

Strategy for Effective International Roll-out must take care of the following issues: variation in infrastructure at regional levels.

- Localized regulatory requirements
- Cultural work preferences
- Language localization needs
- Time zone coverage for support

Factors Constituting Successes

Design for User Experience

Technology in the workplace should ensure:

- Intuitive interface design
- Minimal learning curves
- Seamless integration flows
- Mobile-first access
- Cross-platform consistent experience

Data Security

Platforms that succeed are able to enact;

- Enterprise-grade encryption
- Multi-factor authentication
- Role-based access control
- Audit trail maintenance
- Regular security updates

Scaling Strategy

Growth Plans should take into consideration

- Infrastructure Resilience
- Performance Optimization
- Cost Management
- Support Scalability
- Feature prioritization

What the Future Holds

The future of work technology holds immense promise for those entrepreneurs who will be able to:

- Build solutions that can raise productivity without making it all
- Provide platforms for effective global collaboration.
- Create mechanisms for continuous skill development and adaptation.
- Implement systems that encourage employee wellness and engagement.
- Deploy solutions that protect the privacy of employees while offering real, actionable insights into the organization.

As companies continue to shape and reshape the nature of work, successful entrepreneurs will be those capable of the following:

- Pinpointing explicit pain points from the current work environment
- Developing practical solutions that guarantee measurable improvements
- Developing sustainable business models in concert with organizational objectives
- Develop solid collaborations across the workplace technology ecosystem.
- Ensure flexibility in adjusting to emerging workforce needs.

Business opportunities for workplace technology range from basic productivity tools to holistic solutions for the future of work: entrepreneurs who can match technological innovation with a richly nuanced understanding of the workplace and manage security and privacy standards well will find many growth possibilities opening up.

Success in the space will involve attention to user needs, organizational requirements, and regulatory compliance, all while a commitment to improvement in the work experience is outstanding. As this sector continues to evolve, only the entrepreneurs who will successfully navigate these challenges and deliver measurable improvements to workplace effectiveness are positioned for long-term success.

CHAPTER 5: FINTECH 2.0

Financial technology is moving to another dimension of innovation, while more and more inclusive in the corporate world, achieving easy access, and offering sophisticated solutions with decentralization. This evolution opens many chances for the right entrepreneurs who can manage the complicated crossing of technology, finance, and regulation.

Embedded Finance Solutions

Industry-specific Banking Platforms

The call for customized financial services led to opportunities for vertical-specific banking solutions. Successful startups develop platforms that should be:

- Be integrated seamlessly into the industry workflows
- Assess sector-specific risk
- Lend products customized to their nature
- Facilitate real-time financial monitoring
- Automate industry-specific compliance

These platforms have to balance technological innovation with robust measures related to security while keeping regulatory compliances intact.

Cross-border Payment Optimization

Global commerce is gradually demanding intelligent payment solutions. Key features of a successful platform include:

- Real-time settlement capabilities
- Multi-currency management
- Dynamic optimization of FX
- Automation of regulatory compliance
- Fraud prevention systems

The challenge for entrepreneurs lies in balancing these issues regarding international regulations and providing cost-effective solutions for businesses of all sizes.

Decentralized Finance -Defi- for Business

Supply Chain Financing Solutions

The rise of DeFi opens up new possibilities in supply chain financing platforms for the automation of invoice financing, smart contract payments, peer-to-peer lending, tokenized inventory financing, and dynamic pricing models. In this domain, success requires expertise in both traditional finance and blockchain.

Asset Tokenization Platforms

Digital assets present an opportunity for platforms to create value by providing services in tokenizing real estate, infrastructure project financing, monetizing IP, revenue stream securitization, and fractional ownership management.

These platforms have to balance the complexity of regulatory requirements with market liquidity and security.

Financial Inclusion Tech

Alternative Credit Scoring Systems

Innovation in credit assessment creates an avenue for platforms in the following ways:

- Non-traditional data source analysis
- AI-driven risk assessment
- Real-time creditworthiness updates
- Community-based credit validation
- Allowance for the integration of financial education

All of that requires a careful balance between innovation and fair lending practices, including regulatory compliance.

Micro-lending Platforms for Emerging Markets

Democratization of financial services creates avenues for solutions to enable:

- Mobile-first lending

- Offline transaction capabilities
- Offer flexible payment models
- Offer financial literacy tools
- Allow peer-to-peer lending networks

Market Development Strategies

Complying with regulations

This is vital for successful Fintech platforms in managing:

- Cross-border banking regulations
- Anti-money laundering regulations
- Know Your Customer requirements
- Data privacy provisions
- Consumer protection laws

Security Implementation

The mainstays of security include:

- Multi-tier authentication systems
- Fraud detection in real time
- Data storage with encryption
- Routine security audits
- Incident response policies

Partnership Development

Generally, strategic partnerships are in order with:

- Traditional financial institutions
- Technology providers
- Regulatory bodies
- Industry associations
- Distribution partners

Critical Success Factors and Considerations

User Experience Design

Financial platforms need to focus on:

- Intuitive interface design
- Clear transaction flows
- Transparent fee structures
- Mobile-first access
- Multi-language support

Technical Infrastructure

Robust platforms require:

- High-availability architecture
- Scalable processing capabilities
- Real-time monitoring systems
- Disaster recovery planning
- Flexibility in integration

Market Education

Successful ventures invest in:

- Financial literacy programs
- Product adoption strategies
- User onboarding optimization
- Community engagement
- Trust-building initiatives

Future Outlook

The opportunity of the fintech sector is more worth it to entrepreneurs who can:

- Develop solutions that can solve specific market gaps in financial services
- Create platforms that assure financial inclusion without compromising on security

- Build systems to support cross-border transactions efficiently
- Design solutions to work in harmony with prevailing business processes.
- Deploy a robust compliance framework without compromising on innovation.

Thus, in an ever-evolving financial service, successful entrepreneurs would be the ones who can:

- Identify specific pain points in the existing financial systems;
- Design practical solutions that create measurable impacts;
- Create viable business models that conform to regulatory expectations;
- Forge productive partnerships across the financial value chain;
- Be agile enough to read and adapt to emerging market needs.

The opportunities in Fintech 2.0 embrace solutions beyond just financial services into holistic solutions for the future of finance. Indeed, those entrepreneurs who can merge technological innovation with deep knowledge of financial markets, keeping high standards in terms of security and compliance, will see substantial avenues of growth materialize.

In this space, success involves great attention to regulation, security, and user needs while keeping strong commitments toward better access and efficiency in financial matters. Indeed, how well entrepreneurs can negotiate through the current challenges while delivering value in measurable financial services as the sector evolves will position their businesses for the long haul.

CHAPTER 6: SMART CITY TECHNOLOGIES

The rapid urbanization of the global population, coupled with increasing environmental pressures and constraints on resources, opens unparalleled opportunities for innovations in smart city technologies. Efficiency, sustainability, and an improved quality of life are pursued by cities worldwide, and entrepreneurs are in a very good position to provide transformational solutions across a variety of urban domains.

Solutions for Urban Mobility

Last Mile Delivery Optimization

The explosion of e-commerce and urban delivery services is pressing for intelligent last-mile solutions urgently. Successful start-ups are developing platforms that can:

- Offer real-time routing planning
- Coordinate multi-modal delivery networks
- Develop micro-fulfillment center management
- Offer integrations for autonomous delivery
- Track metrics on environmental impact

Efficiency in the development and adaptation to diverse urban environments will have to be balanced with sustainability in these platforms.

Public Transport Integration Platforms

The rise of autonomous mobility presents opportunities to develop platforms focused on:
- Traffic flow optimization
- Vehicle-to-infrastructure communication
- Smart parking management
- Public transport integration
- Safety monitoring systems

Success is actualized by sophisticated integration capabilities while ensuring the robustness of safety standards.

Intelligent Infrastructure Management

IoT-based Utility Optimization

Digitization in city infrastructure opens a way to solutions that:
- Monitor the consumption of resources in real-time
- Forecast maintenance and repair needs
- Optimize energy distribution
- Help manage water supply systems with efficiency
- Support smart grid integration

To do so successfully, it requires both sensor networks and a variety of advanced analytics that turn data into insight.

Urban Planning Analytics

Data-driven urban planning opens possibilities for platforms offering:
- Analysis of population flow
- Patterns of usage of infrastructure
- Environmental impact and footprint assessment
- Development scenarios modeling
- Public space optimization

These solutions must balance technical sophistication with practical applicability for the urban planner.

Community Engagement and Local Economy

The desired outcomes will be community engagement platforms and enabling of local commerce. Revitalization of the local economy will be facilitated by platforms that can:
- Connect local businesses with residents
- Enable the creation of digital marketplaces
- Support community currencies
- Implement loyalty programs
- Track impact metrics for economic contribution

To succeed, it is necessary to create inclusive solutions to serve the diverse needs of the community.

Implementation Strategies

Infrastructure Integration

Successful smart city solutions should take into account the following key factors:
- Legacy system compatibility
- Scalability needs
- Standards for data integration
- Security protocols
- Maintenance procedures

Stakeholder Management

Engagement with the various stakeholders involves:
- Municipal authorities

- Utility providers
- Business communities
- Resident groups
- Technology partners

Data Governance

A well-functioning data management framework provides for:
- Privacy protection
- Data ownership
- Standards for security
- Protocols for sharing
- Compliance obligations

Success Factors and Considerations

Technical Architecture

Some of the successful platforms have implemented the following:
- Open standards
- Modular architecture
- Scalable infrastructure
- Protocols for interoperability
- Real-time processing capabilities

User Experience

The various solutions should focus on:
- Intuitive interface
- Universal access
- Multi-language support
- Optimization for mobile

- Offline functionality

Sustainability Integration

All environmental considerations entail:
- Energy efficiency
- Resource optimization
- Emissions reduction
- Waste management
- Circular economy principles

Future Outlook

The field of smart city technologies provides fertile ground for entrepreneurs who can:

1. Develop solutions for specific urban challenges
2. Create platforms to increase the efficiency of the city while improving its livability
3. Build systems to foster community involvement
4. Design solutions for environmental sustainability
5. Apply frameworks to protect privacy, yet also enable innovation

With urban evolvement, successful entrepreneurs will be those able to:
- Identify major pain points in the urban system
- Offer practical solutions leading to measurable improvement
- Develop viable business models in line with municipal objectives
- Create strong partnerships among a wide range of players within the urban ecosystem
- Maintain flexibility toward changing city needs over time

Smart city technologies will create opportunities that go from individual solutions to whole urban transformations. Key areas for future innovation include:

- Integrated mobility solutions
- Resilient infrastructure systems
- Community-led development
- Monitoring and protection of the environment
- Digital Democracy

The frontier that calls for critical entrepreneurial innovation in terms of creating an impact in building sustainable businesses is the smart city technology vertical. It requires an optimum mix of technological capability, stakeholder engagement, and environmental responsibility while keeping the focus on improving the quality of urban life.

CHAPTER 7: EVOLUTION IN EDUCATION TECHNOLOGY

The adoption of technology in education has rapidly accelerated, affording unparalleled opportunities for innovation in the delivery of learning, assessment, and building skills. Around the world, education systems are adapting to shifting workforce needs and technological capabilities, and entrepreneurs are well-positioned to transform how people learn and develop skills throughout their lifetime.

Personalized Learning Platforms

AI-driven Curriculum Adaptation

The interest in personalized learning experiences has opened avenues for systems that:
- Analyze individual learning patterns
- Adjust the difficulty of content in real-time
- Identify and fill knowledge gaps
- Optimize learning pathways
- Monitor comprehension and retention

These platforms must balance sophisticated analytics with pragmatic pedagogy and keep learners engaged.

Competency-Based Learning Pathways

The move toward competency-based learning opens up new doors for solutions such as:

- A line-of-sight into career pathways, mapping relevant skills
- Digital modular progression and learning pathways
- Real-world application scenarios
- Metrics of acquired skills
- Issue verifiable skill credentials

In all of this, deep connectivity with industry while maintaining educational rigor will be key to success.

Upskilling Corporate Solutions

Micro-credentialing Platforms

The rapid evolution of workplace skills requires new approaches to certification, including industry-aligned skill verification, stackable credential systems, real-time assessment methods, portfolio development tools, and employer validation frameworks. These platforms are envisioned to meet the needs of access while preserving the values of credibility and maintaining industrially relevant standards.

Real-time Competency Gap Analysis

The workforce development process demands sophisticated systems and tools to keep watch on industry trends, organizational capability assessment, identification of emerging new skill requirements, customized learning plan design, and monitoring of metrics related to workforce readiness. Success will be achieved by developing and combining labor market insights with practical learning solutions.

Education Metaverse Use Cases

Virtual Labs

Practical learning creates opportunities for platforms that offer immersive experiment simulations, real-time collaboration tools, data collection and analysis, training in safety procedures, and sharing resources across institutions. Such solutions need to balance technological sophistication with educational effectiveness.

Immersive Learning Environments

Next-generation learning environments will offer:
- Interactive 3D visualizations
- Virtual field trips
- Collaborative problem-solving
- Scenario-based learning
- Cultural immersion experiences

Implementation Strategies

Integration within Educational Institutions

Any successful Edtech solution must address:
- Compatibility with existing systems
- Assessment framework alignment
- Training requirements of teachers
- Integration into administrative workflows
- Data management protocols

Corporate Learning Integration

The effective delivery of learning at the workplace requires:
- Alignment with business processes
- Integration into performance metrics
- Career pathing and mapping
- ROI measurement

- Compliance tracking

Access and Equity

Holistic approaches must address:
- Diverse learning styles
- Language barriers
- Tech limitations
- Cultural adaptability
- Special education needs

Success Factors and Considerations

Pedagogical Architecture

Efficient platforms enable:
- Evidence-based learning
- Engagement optimization
- Knowledge retention strategies
- Progress monitoring
- Adaptive feedback systems

Technical Infrastructure

Robust solutions require:
- Scalable architecture
- Mobile optimization
- Offline capability
- Flexible integration
- Security protocols

Data Analytics

Success depends upon:
- Advanced learning analytics
- Predictive modeling
- Performance tracking
- Impact assessment
- Measuring outcomes

The Future

The education technology marketplace holds tremendous promise for entrepreneurs who can create solutions that raise the bar on learning outcomes while retaining engagement. Key focus areas include:

1. Development of lifelong skills development platforms
2. Creation of mechanisms for global knowledge sharing
3. Implementation of inclusive education pathways
4. Development of robust learning outcome assessment frameworks

To succeed, entrepreneurs must:
- Identify specific gaps in current educational systems
- Offer pragmatic solutions with measurable learning effects
- Develop sustainable business models
- Foster excellent partnerships within the education ecosystem
- Maintain flexibility in adapting to evolving learning needs

The educational technology opportunities extend beyond traditional academic settings into comprehensive lifelong learning solutions. Entrepreneurs who connect technological innovation with deep learning process insight, combined with sound pedagogical standards, will see tremendous opportunities for scale.

Key areas for future innovation include:

- Adaptive learning systems
- Competency-based certification
- Immersive learning environments
- Workplace learning integration
- Global access to education

Success in the sector will require a focus on learning outcomes, user engagement, and measurement of impact while maintaining a rigorous commitment to educational quality. As this sector continues to develop, entrepreneurs who understand these constraints while delivering measurable value in improved learning outcomes will thrive.

CHAPTER 8: AGRICULTURE AND FOOD TECHNOLOGY

The intersection of technology with agriculture and food production represents one of the most crucial frontiers of innovation in our time. Global food systems face unprecedented pressure due to population growth, climate change impacts, and demands for sustainable production. These challenges present entrepreneurs with extraordinary opportunities to revolutionize how we produce, process, and distribute food.

Precision Agriculture Solutions

Autonomous Farming Systems

The evolution of agricultural automation has created the demand for platforms that enable:
- Management of autonomous equipment fleets
- Field operations optimization
- Real-time crop health monitoring
- Precision irrigation management
- Automated harvest timing

These systems must strike a balance between technological sophistication and practical farming realities.

Crop Optimization Platforms

Data-driven agriculture requires solutions offering:
- Predictive yield modeling

- Disease outbreak forecasting
- Nutrient management optimization
- Weather impact analysis
- Resource allocation planning

Success in this area depends on combining deep agricultural expertise with advanced analytics.

Alternative Protein Technologies

Lab-grown Meat Optimization

Cellular agriculture creates opportunities for platforms specializing in:
- Production process automation
- Quality control systems
- Scale-up optimization
- Cost-reduction strategies
- Regulatory compliance management

While promising, these platforms must address both technological and consumer acceptance challenges.

Plant-based Food Innovation

The plant-based industry seeks solutions for:
- Ingredient optimization
- Texture enhancement
- Nutritional profiling
- Production scaling
- Shelf life extension

Success requires balancing taste and texture with nutritional requirements.

Food Supply Chain Transparency

Farm-to-Table Traceability

Consumer demand for transparency creates opportunities for platforms offering:
- Product origin and journey tracking
- Storage condition monitoring
- Sustainability claim verification
- Recall management
- Consumer Transparency

These solutions must balance comprehensive tracking with practical implementation.

Quality Assurance Systems

Food safety requirements drive demand for platforms providing:
- Real-time contamination detection
- Temperature monitoring
- Compliance documentation
- Supplier verification
- Risk assessment automation

Implementation Strategies

Agricultural Integration

Successful Agtech solutions must consider:
- Existing farming practices
- Seasonal variations
- Equipment compatibility
- Labor skill levels
- Local infrastructure limitations

Supply Chain Optimization

Effective deployment requires attention to:
- Storage requirements
- Transportation logistics
- Processing capabilities
- Distribution networks
- Retail integration

Sustainability Integration

Environmental considerations include:
- Water usage optimization
- Carbon footprint reduction
- Waste minimization
- Biodiversity protection
- Soil health management

Success Factors and Considerations

Technical Architecture

Robust platforms should focus on:
- IoT sensor networks
- Data analytics capabilities
- Machine learning models
- Mobile accessibility
- Offline functionality

User Experience

Solutions must be prioritized:

- Intuitive interfaces
- Practical utility
- Local language support
- Remote location access
- Training requirements

Regulatory Compliance

Success depends on managing:
- Food safety standards
- Environmental regulations
- Labor requirements
- Export Compliance
- Certification processes

Future Outlook

Agriculture and food technology offer significant opportunities for entrepreneurs who can:
- Provide solutions enhancing production efficiency and sustainability
- Develop platforms for food safety monitoring and transparency
- Design supply chain optimization systems
- Create solutions for resource constraints
- Implement sustainability frameworks

As global food systems evolve, successful entrepreneurs will:
- Identify critical food system challenges
- Create practical solutions driving measurable improvements
- Develop industry-compatible sustainable business models
- Build strong partnerships across the food value chain
- Adapt to changing climate conditions

Key areas for future innovation include:
- Vertical farming systems
- Precision fermentation
- Smart irrigation solutions
- Waste reduction technologies
- Alternative protein development

The opportunities span from individual solutions to system-wide transformation in agriculture and food technology. Entrepreneurs who combine technological innovation with deep agricultural understanding while maintaining strong sustainability standards are well-positioned for growth. Success requires careful consideration of food security, environmental impact, economic viability, social responsibility, and technical feasibility.

The sector's continuous evolution creates unique opportunities for those who can navigate these challenges while delivering quantifiable improvements in food production and distribution. The combination of advanced technologies with traditional agricultural knowledge enables innovations that can address both local and global food system challenges.

CHAPTER 9: NEW IOT AND SMART MANUFACTURING

The integration of the Industrial Internet of Things with advanced manufacturing approaches is revolutionizing production systems worldwide. Whereas industries are struggling to cope with this fourth industrial revolution, such an opportunity has been presented to entrepreneurs to develop solutions to enhance efficiency, resilience, and sustainability in manufacturing operations.

Intelligent Factory Solutions

Predictive Maintenance Platforms

New Emerging Strategies for Maintenance open up new vistas for platforms that can:

- Monitor real-time health of equipment
- Predict imminent failure
- Optimized scheduling of maintenance
- Component lifecycle tracking
- ROI calculation of maintenance

The analytics on these platforms have to be sophisticated yet meet practical implementation requirements.

Digital Twin Technologies

Manufacturing optimization requires an all-rounded digital twin solution in:

- Creation of accurate virtual representations
- Allowing simulations in real-time
- Optimization of processes
- Planning Scenarios
- Tracking performance indicators

This requires deep integration while ensuring system reliability.

Supply Chain Resilience Technology

Risk Assessment Systems

Vulnerability within global supply chains calls for platforms that avail the following:
- Real-time monitoring of risk
- Assessing the impact of disruption
- Optimizing alternative routes
- Optimizing stock levels
- Early warning systems

These solutions must balance comprehensive coverage with actionable insights.

Alternate Supplier Discovery

Supply chain diversification demands platforms that:
- Identify qualified suppliers
- Assess supplier capabilities
- Evaluate financial stability
- Monitor performance metrics
- Enable onboarding processes

Success will depend on a detailed analysis of suppliers with matching implementation support.

Manufacturing Marketplace Platforms

Capacity Sharing Solutions

Resource optimization creates opportunities for platforms that enable:
- Matching of production capacity
- Coordinating equipment sharing
- Demand forecasting
- Cost optimization
- Quality assurance management

These shall address both the technical and trust-related aspects.

On-demand Manufacturing Networks

The evolution of manufacturing flexibility requires platforms that would offer:
- Rapid prototyping services
- Production capacity matching
- Quality control systems
- Logistics coordination
- Cost optimization

Implementation Strategies

Factory Integration

- Legacy system compatibility
- Network Infrastructure
- Security requirements
- Training needs of staff
- Maintenance procedures

Data Management

- Real-time processing
- Optimization of storage
- Security protocols
- Analytics standards
- Standards for integration

Change Management

- Workforce adaptation
- Process modification
- Development of skills
- Cultural change
- Performance measurement

Technical Considerations

Technical Architecture

A robust platform should implement:
- Edge computing capabilities
- Cloud integration
- Security frameworks
- Scalable infrastructure
- Redundancy systems

User Experience

Solutions must be designed to showcase:
- Operator-friendly interfaces
- Mobile accessibility
- Real-time visibility
- Alert management
- Remote monitoring

Security Implementation

Critical security measures will include:
- Network segmentation
- Access control
- Threat detection
- Incident response
- Compliance management

Outlook

The industrial IoT and manufacturing is a great area for entrepreneurs who can develop solutions to make op
erations more efficient with maintained reliability. This includes developing platforms that enhance the resiliency of the supply chain, building systems that will enable resources to be optimized, designing solutions to promote sustainable manufacturing, or implementing frameworks that will protect sensitive industrial data.

Future Success Factors

The successful entrepreneur will be able to:
- Identify concrete pain points in the current manufacturing systems

- Develop pragmatic solutions that have measurable improvements
- Create sustainable business models that offer solutions to industry needs
- Strong partnership with all participants in the manufacturing chain
- Flexibility to adjust according to the evolving standards of technology

Key Innovation Areas

Future innovation will focus on:
- Advanced automation systems
- Sustainable manufacturing processes
- Supply chain optimization
- Automation of quality control
- Energy efficiency solutions

Opportunities in IoT and manufacturing reach beyond point solutions to complete digital transformation. Therefore, entrepreneurs who can correctly merge technological innovation with deep knowledge about manufacturing processes, while maintaining high standards of security, will see enormous opportunities for growth.

Critical Success Factors

Success in this space calls for due consideration of the following aspects:
- Operational requirements
- Technical feasibility
- Economic viability
- Security considerations
- Regulatory compliance

With this ever-shifting industry, an entrepreneur finding a way around such challenges and being able to create measurable improvement in the manufacturing operations is well placed for long-term success. The fusion of state-of-the-art technologies with traditional manufacturing expertise brings very special opportunities for innovation that are able to address pressing local and global industrial challenges.

CHAPTER 10: NEW CONSUMER TECHNOLOGY

The boundary between the physical and digital worlds continues to blur, creating unique opportunities for entrepreneurs to transform how consumers engage, purchase, and manage their digital lives. These innovations in consumer technology are reshaping consumer behavior, technologies, and expectations of digital experiences.

Social Commerce Solutions

AR/VR Shopping Platforms

Immersive commerce platforms are emerging with capabilities for:
- Virtual try-ons of products
- Immersive shopping experiences
- 3D product visualization
- Spatial commerce experience
- Key engagement metrics tracking

These platforms must balance technological sophistication with practical usability.

Community-driven Marketplace

Social shopping platforms require:
- Integration capabilities for influencers
- User-generated content management
- Real-time social proof

- Community engagement tools
- Performance analytics

Success depends on seamlessly integrating social dynamics with commerce operations.

Digital Identity Management

Privacy-first Personal Data Vaults

Privacy-focused solutions should provide:
- Secure personal information storage
- Selective data sharing controls
- Consent preference management
- Digital footprint tracking
- Breach notifications

Credential Verification Systems

Digital trust platforms must offer:
- Digital credential verification
- Identity attestation management
- Secure authentication
- Regulatory compliance support
- Cross-platform verification

Wellness Tech Platforms

Holistic Health Tracking

Integrated wellness platforms should feature:
- Multi-parameter health monitoring
- Lifestyle pattern analysis
- Personalized recommendations

- Health provider interfaces
- Wellness goal tracking

Personal Development Analytics

Self-improvement solutions should include:
- Personal goal tracking
- Behavior pattern analysis
- Progress metrics
- Habit formation tools
- Improvement insights generation

Implementation Strategies

User Adoption

Key focus areas:
- Onboarding ease
- Value demonstration
- Trust building
- Community engagement
- Retention optimization

Privacy Protection

Essential elements:
- Data minimization
- Encryption standards
- User control options
- Transparency measures
- Compliance frameworks

Platform Integration

Critical factors:
- Device compatibility
- API connectivity
- Third-party integrations
- Cross-platform sync
- Performance optimization

Success Factors and Considerations

User Experience Design

Priorities include:
- Intuitive interfaces
- Seamless interactions
- Personalization options
- Mobile-first design
- Accessibility features

Technical Architecture

Essential components:
- Scalable systems
- Real-time processing
- Data security
- Cloud integration
- Performance monitoring

Market Positioning

Key elements:
- Brand differentiation
- Value proposition

- Target audience
- Pricing strategy
- Growth metrics

Future Outlook

The consumer technology industry presents significant opportunities for entrepreneurs to:
- Create privacy-focused solutions
- Build meaningful social connection platforms
- Develop personal growth systems
- Design digital wellbeing solutions
- Implement secure data frameworks

Future innovation platforms will focus on:
- Immersive experiences
- Privacy-enhancing technologies
- Personalized wellness
- Digital identity
- Community-driven platforms

Success in this sector will depend on:
- User experience excellence
- Privacy protection
- Technological reliability
- Social responsibility
- Ethical considerations

Entrepreneurs who can successfully integrate technological innovation with consumer behavior understanding while maintaining robust data privacy standards will find significant growth opportunities. The future belongs to those who can meet these challenges while delivering superior value to consumers, opening new possibilities for innovative solutions to personal and societal challenges.

CHAPTER 11: VIRTUAL REALITY & AUGMENTED REALITY

In an era where virtual and augmented reality technologies are reaching maturity, entrepreneurs face unprecedented opportunities to reshape human interaction with digital information and experiences. The convergence of hardware advancement, software innovation, and growing market acceptance creates fertile ground for ventures harnessing these transformative technologies.

Innovative Applications in VR/AR

Remote Work and Collaboration

The development of virtual workspaces enables:
- Truly immersive team meetings
- 3D product design reviews
- Virtual training programs
- Collaboration spaces
- Spatial computing interfaces

Success in this domain requires balancing technological possibilities with practical business needs.

Interactive Training and Education

Modern learning experiences demand platforms that provide:

- Immersive skill development
- Complex scenario simulation
- Real-time performance feedback
- Multi-user training environments
- Progress analytics

Success in this area requires combining pedagogical expertise with immersive technology capabilities.

Scaling VR/AR: Challenges Ahead

Hardware-Software Integration

Key considerations include:
- Cross-platform compatibility
- Performance optimization
- Device management
- Content delivery systems
- User interaction standards

These challenges demand advanced technical solutions while maintaining user accessibility.

Strategic Partnerships

Market development requires collaboration with:
- Hardware manufacturers
- Content creators
- Distribution platforms
- Industry specialists
- Technology providers

Market Differentiation Strategies

Industry-Specific Solutions

Vertical market opportunities include:
- Healthcare simulation
- Industrial training
- Retail visualization
- Real estate tours
- Entertainment experiences

Each application requires deep domain expertise alongside technical capabilities.

Innovative Customer Experience

Competitive advantage depends on:
- User comfort optimization
- Intuitive interactions
- Content quality
- Performance Reliability
- Support systems

Implementation Considerations

Technical Architecture

Robust platforms require:
- Scalable rendering systems
- Low latency networking
- Asset optimization
- Cloud integration
- Security frameworks

User Experience Design

Success factors include:
- Motion comfort
- Interface clarity
- Natural interaction
- Visual quality
- Audio integration

Content Management

Effective solutions must address:
- Asset creation workflows
- Content distribution
- Version control
- Quality assurance
- Update management

Success Factors and Market Development

Technical Innovation

Key capabilities include:
- Real-time rendering
- Spatial computing
- Hand tracking
- Environmental mapping
- Multi-user synchronization

Business Model Optimization

Sustainable growth requires:

- Clear value proposition
- Revenue model alignment
- Cost structure management
- Market penetration strategy
- Scaling framework

Industry Partnership Development

Success depends on:
- Hardware ecosystem relationships
- Content creator networks
- Distribution channel partnerships
- Enterprise client engagement
- Technology vendor collaboration

Future Outlook

The VR/AR industry presents significant opportunities for entrepreneurs who can:
- Develop solutions for specific industry pain points
- Create platforms for smooth immersive experiences
- Build effective training and education systems
- Enhance remote collaboration
- Ensure consistent performance

Key areas of future development include:
- Mixed reality applications
- Spatial computation
- Haptic feedback systems
- Neural interfaces
- Environmental scanning

Critical success factors encompass:
- User comfort and safety
- Technical performance
- Content quality
- Integration capabilities
- Market Timing

As the sector matures, entrepreneurs who successfully address these challenges while providing meaningful user value will find significant long-term success. The integration of VR/AR technologies with mainstream business processes continues to create unique opportunities for innovation across multiple industries.

CHAPTER 12: AUTONOMOUS & INTELLIGENT TRANSPORTATION

Transportation systems are being transformed in view of developments in autonomous technology, artificial intelligence, and connected infrastructure. This evolution creates unparalleled opportunities for innovation and entrepreneurial spirit to re-engineer the mobility system and offer solutions to urban and long-distance transport needs.

Future of Autonomous Driving

Advanced AI for Operations of Vehicles

The development of autonomous systems makes it possible to develop platforms for:

- Real-time decision optimization
- Enhancement of perception systems
- Enhanced navigation accuracy
- V2V management
- Enable predictive safety

These solutions must strike a balance between technological sophistication and absolute safety requirements.

Logistics and Public Transport Applications

The transformation underway in commercial transport demands platforms capable of delivering:
- Fleet optimization algorithms
- Route planning systems
- Predictive maintenance
- Energy efficiency management
- Passenger flow optimization

Here, success is ensured by marrying operational efficiency with regulatory compliance.

Intelligent Transportation Solutions

Real-time Transportation Data Platforms

Urban mobility optimization creates avenues for solutions directed at:
- Integration of multiple modes of transport
- Analysis of traffic congestion patterns
- Demand fluctuation prediction
- Dynamic pricing
- System performance monitoring

They have to strike a balance between broad coverage and actionable insights.

Smart Last-mile Delivery

What the future of delivery services will expect from such systems is the capability to:
- Coordinate autonomous vehicles
- Optimize delivery routes
- Manage pickup/drop-off points
- Secure package handling

- Monitor delivery performance

Key Strategic Considerations

Regulatory Requirements

Implementation will involve managing:
- Safety Certifications
- Operational Permits
- Insurance compliance
- Data protection
- Environmental standards

Local Government Partnerships

Effective deployment will involve:
- Infrastructure coordination
- Policy Alignment
- Public Engagements
- Safety protocols
- Performance monitoring

Implementation Strategies

Technical Architecture

Competitive systems will have:
- Sensor Fusion Capabilities
- Edge Computing Infrastructure
- Real-time processing
- Redundancy systems
- Security frameworks

Safety Implementation

Some key safety features that will be implemented are:
- Fail-safe systems
- Emergency protocols
- Risk Assessment
- Monitoring performance
- Incident response

User Experience Design

Success will depend upon attention to:
- Interface Access
- Service Reliability
- Customer communications
- Safety Awareness
- Trust development

Market Development Considerations

Infrastructure Integration

Solutions will have to successfully account for:
- Charging networks
- Communications systems
- Maintenance facilities
- Data networks
- Physical infrastructure

Stakeholder Management

Successful deployment will depend on consultation with:

- Regulatory authorities
- Insurers
- Technology partners
- Public stakeholders
- Infrastructure operators

Economic Viability

Long-term viable operations will have to be concerned with:
- Costs of operations
- Revenue maximization
- Investment in infrastructure
- Efficient maintenance
- Scale economy

Future Outlook

The autonomous vehicle and intelligent transport sector can have great promise for those entrepreneurs who will be able to:
1. Develop solutions that can enhance safety while improving efficiency
2. Create a facilitation platform that allows seamless mobility integration
3. Design systems to facilitate sustainable transport
4. Provide solutions to utilize resources efficiently
5. Implement regulatory compliance frameworks

As transportation systems continue to evolve, the entrepreneurs likely to succeed will be those who can:
- Pinpoint specific mobility issues in diverse markets
- Come up with practical solutions that have measurable impacts
- Initiate viable businesses that meet public demand

- Establish solid relationships along the value chain in transportation
- Be resilient in adjusting to changes in regulation

Key areas where significant innovations are foreseen to happen in the near future include:
- Autonomous electric vehicles
- Smart infrastructure
- Smart traffic management

The technology of autonomous driving will be part of a system of comprehensive mobility, such as platforms Mobility-as-a-Service, to provide environmentally friendly transportation solutions. It is here, on this opportunistic platform, that entrepreneurs might address technological innovation with profound insight into the needs of transportation while considering the high standards of safety.

Critical Success Factors

- Safety-first approach
- Scalable technology
- Regulatory alignment
- Public acceptance
- Economic viability

Perhaps no other area in the next decade holds as much potential for entrepreneurial innovation as the transformation of transportation via autonomous and smart technologies. To be sure, success in this space requires a delicate balance among technological capability, safety considerations, and public trust—concurrently keeping in focus the goals of enhancing access to transportation and efficiency.

CHAPTER 13: BLOCKCHAIN AND WEB3 STARTUPS

The landscape of blockchain technology and Web3 ventures is highly dynamic and continuously changing, which presents extraordinary opportunities, along with unique challenges, to entrepreneurs. This chapter will discuss the most promising areas of blockchain-based startups and give strategic insights into how to build successful ventures in this dynamic space.

Blockchain for Business Solutions

Enterprise adoption of blockchain technology has moved beyond experimental phases into pragmatic implementation, opening an entire world of opportunities for startups. More and more organizations have begun to realize the potential that blockchain possesses to revolutionize traditional ways of doing business through greater transparency, security, and efficiency.

Supply Chain Management Revolution

Supply chain management is one of the most mature use cases for blockchain technology. Startups are developing solutions that address some very critical pain points in international supply chains:

- End-to-End Visibility: The transparency provided by blockchain-based platforms, as in real-time, location-based tracking of goods from origin to their intended destination, allows the creation of tamper-proof records. It promotes accountability and reduces disputes.

- Authenticity Verification: Solutions running on blockchain act as a weapon in the anti-counterfeiting battle because they can prove that something is real. Some industries where it is necessary include pharmaceuticals and luxury goods.
- Smart Contract Integration: With smart contracts, the automation of executed contracts will help facilitate frictionless relations with suppliers and cut overhead administration to allow timely payments.

Enterprise-Grade Decentralized Applications

The market space for enterprise-oriented decentralized applications is growing further into areas like document authentication, cross-border trade finance, and the tokenization of assets. These include:

- Document Authentication: Secured verification systems for legal documents, certificates, and corporate records.
- Cross-Border Trade Finance: Platforms that facilitate international trade by reducing paperwork and accelerating processes using blockchain-driven letters of credit and bills of lading.
- Asset Tokenization: Solutions to allow multiple owners of real-world assets, including but not limited to real estate and intellectual property.

Trends in Web3 Adoption

The Web3 ecosystem is one of rapid evolution, where new models of user engagement and value creation emerge with great regularity.

Decentralized Social and Creator Economies

The movement into decentralized social platforms represents a very fundamental shift in the way online communities interact:

- Content Ownership: Platforms enabling creators to retain ownership and monetize their content with token-based systems.
- Community Governance: Solutions allowing users to contribute to decision-making processes concerning a platform through DAOs.
- Reputation Systems: Blockchain verification of online identity and achievements, creating a portable digital reputation.

The Use of NFTs Beyond Digital Art

While digital art was the dominant early conversation around NFTs, the technology is beginning to find real business applications in the following ways:

- Brand Engagement: The use of NFTs by companies for customer loyalty programs in terms of access to products or services.
- Digital Rights Management: How to manage and monetize intellectual property rights using NFTs.
- Event Access: Those applications that involve NFTs for event ticketing and control, be that a virtual or a physical event.

Challenges and Opportunities

Success in the blockchain and Web3 ecosystem involves several critical considerations.

Trust in Decentralized Systems

Trust is one of the most central issues in decentralized systems:

- Security Implication: High security through the use of multi-signature wallets, key management that's safe, and regular auditing of smart contracts.

- User Experience: Ease-of-use interfaces abstracting blockchain intricacies while allowing transparency and security.
- Community Building: A focus on active user communities and effective governance mechanisms that ensure their sustainability.

Regulatory Compliance and Data Privacy

The blockchain and Web3 legal landscape is in a state of near-continuous evolution:

- Jurisdictional Considerations: Understand and regularly adjust to the diverse and changing regulatory demands across multiple jurisdictions.
- Data Protection: Offer solutions that implement data protection in a privacy-enhanced manner, with conformance to global data protection regulations.
- KYC/AML Integration: Balance decentralization with necessary compliance requirements for customer due diligence.

Sustainability and Scalability

Long-term success will be built on creating sustainable and scalable solutions by keeping in mind the following angles:

- Environmental Impact: The efficiency of the consensus mechanisms and carbon-neutral operation in order to overcome the energy consumption concern.
- Technical Scalability: Using layer-2 solutions, cross-chain interoperability for increased throughput.
- Business Model Innovation: Making the hard road toward sustainable, non-decentralization-undermining revenue models.

Key Strategic Recommendations for Entrepreneurs

1. Focus on real problems and don't try to solve business issues that might well not require blockchain in the first place.
2. Build interoperability so that the solutions can connect with existing systems and other blockchain networks.
3. Educate: Use some resources to educate potential users and stakeholders about the benefits of blockchain and how to use this technology.
4. Plan for compliance: embed regulatory compliance at the heart of solutions, rather than treating it as an afterthought.
5. Be flexible: With regular updating based on changing standards of technology and regulatory needs, do not lose the sense of core value propositions.

There is still immense opportunity in the blockchain and Web3 space for innovative startups. However, success involves a proper balance between technical leads with strong business acumen and regulatory needs understanding. In the maturing ecosystem, only those startups that focus on problem-solving with sustainable and compliant solution-building are more likely to see long-term success.

CHAPTER 14: DEEP TECH OPPORTUNITIES

Deep technology is, arguably, one of the most exciting and revolutionary growth opportunities for any startup of the modern era. Three key points of discussion in this chapter are quantum computing, robotics automation, and advanced materials technology.

Quantum Computing Applications

The Quantum Computing space is rapidly evolving from a theoretical promise to practical implementation, carrying many opportunities with it for startups in developing industry-specific solutions.

Industry-Specific Quantum Algorithms

The ongoing work in developing quantum algorithms provides immense scope for industry-specific applications including:
- Financial Services: Portfolio Optimization and Risk Analysis form the parts of quantum algorithms, leading to exponential performances enabled by complex financial models that fall well beyond the capabilities of classical computing systems.
- Drug Discovery: Molecular Simulation Algorithms by a significant factor accelerate the drug development pipeline by modeling chemical interactions at a quantum level.
- Weather Modeling: Sophisticated algorithms process complex climate data to enhance weather forecasts and model future climate change.

Quantum-Safe Security Solutions

The increased capability of quantum computing increases the bar on quantum-resistant security measures, which become ever more critical:
- Post-Quantum Cryptography: Methods of encryption resistant against both quantum and classical computing attacks are developed.
- Quantum Key Distribution: Secure communication systems using the principles of quantum mechanics to detect any interference with the key exchange process.
- Hybrid Security Frameworks: Solutions that combine classical and quantum-safe approaches for comprehensive security during the transition period.

Robotics Automation Platforms

The Robotics sector is recording extremely rapid growth, stirred by advancements in AI, sensor technology, and material sciences.

Collaborative Robot Management

The growing use of cobots will drive a series of opportunities for platforms that enable:
- Intuitive Programming: Visual programming interfaces that let nontechnical users program robot behaviors.
- Safety Integration: Advanced sensor systems and AI enabling safe human-robot collaboration in shared workspaces.
- Adaptive Learning: Systems that enable robots to learn from human demonstrations and adjust their behavior for fits.

Robot-as-a-Service Solutions

The democratization of robotics by way of service-based models opens new dimensions in the following ways:

- Flexible Deployment: Subscription-based robot deployment models that will reduce the capital expenditure requirement for businesses.
- Industry-Specific Applications: Specialized robotics solutions for sectors like agriculture, health care, and logistics.
- Performance Analytics: Real-time monitoring and optimization of operations in robotic platforms.

Advanced Materials Technology

The innovation in the field of materials science opens new perspectives in many industries—from building construction to the manufacturing of electronics.

Sustainable Material Development

The drive for sustainability is pushing innovation in the realm of material development:
- Bio-Based Materials: New material development out of renewable feedstocks, decreasing reliance on petrochemicals.
- Recycling Technologies: Advanced processes in taking down existing materials and repurposing them.
- Carbon-Negative Materials: Material that during processing or use captures carbon dioxide.

Application of Smart Materials

New functionalities bring intelligence to materials, including:
- Self-Healing Material: Materials that are in essence self-healing when damage has occurred, extending the life of the products.
- Responsive Surfaces: Materials changing properties due to environmental conditions.
- Energy-Efficient Materials: Advanced materials enlarge energy efficiency in buildings and devices.

Implementation Strategies and Challenges

Deep tech's success needs a careful assessment of many critical factors.

Research and Development

Deep tech startups need an effective R&D strategy through:
- Academic Partnerships: Collaboration with universities and research institutions for accessing advanced research facilities.
- IP Strategy: Comprehensive protection of intellectual property to competitively advantage the company.
- Validation Process: Thorough validation and testing of technologies against standard conditions.

Commercialization Pathways

Deep tech innovations need the following to translate into products:
- Market Timing: Understanding the maturity of the technology vs. the timing of the market.
- Industry Partnerships: Strategic collaboration with established players to support market entry.
- Scalability Planning: Well-detailed, step-by-step roadmap from prototype to commercial production.

Funding Considerations

Deep tech ventures usually involve heavy capital investment:
- Patient Capital: Identifying investors who understand the longer development cycles in deep tech.
- Public Funding: Government grants and opportunities for research funding to be highly leveraged.

- Milestone-Based Funding: Securing funding rounds against clear technical and commercial milestones.

Strategic Recommendations for Deep Tech Entrepreneurs

For entrepreneurs venturing into the deep tech space, consider the following:

1. Problem-Solution Fit: The technology needs to solve serious market needs and not be in search of problems to solve
2. Strong Technical Teams: Hire and retain top talent with specialized experience in relevant technical domains
3. Clear IP Strategy: Invest early in their development process in comprehensive protection of intellectual property
4. Allow for Realistic Timeline: Plan and budget for long cycles of development and validation
5. Develop a Capital Efficiency Plan: Devise strategies for deploying resources efficiently over longer development times

Deep tech still abounds with opportunities for startups, which face their unique set of challenges. Success here needs technical excellence, strategic business planning, and resource management. In fact, as such technologies mature, effective bridging of the chasm between breakthrough innovation and practical implementation will best position startups to create substantial value and impact.

Where quantum computing meets robotics and advanced materials, new opportunities that have never been dreamed of are now possible. Those entrepreneurs who can harness these technologies toward solving real-world problems will be at the leading edge of determining the shape of the future not only of industry but also of society.

CHAPTER 15: BUILDING A FUTURE-PROOF STARTUP

In an era of unmatched technological advancement and market volatility, building a future-proof startup requires more than just state-of-the-art technology or an exciting product. This chapter explores the fundamental elements needed to create resilient, sustainable, and globally competitive startups that can successfully evolve within dynamic enterprise environments.

Strategic Positioning

The foundation of a future-proof startup lies in its strategic positioning within the market ecosystem. This positioning must be robust enough to face current challenges while maintaining flexibility for future changes.

Considerations of Market Timing

Successful market timing balances several key factors:

Assessment of Market Readiness

- Assessment of customer pain points and willingness to adopt new solutions
- Analysis of supporting infrastructure and maturity of technology
- Regulatory environment assessment and compliance requirements

Competition Analysis

- Identification of direct and indirect competitors
- Market saturation points
- Potential market entrants from adjacent sectors

Resource Availability

- Access to required talent and expertise
- Ready availability of technologies and partnerships
- Availability of ecosystem-supporting elements

Building Competitive Moats

Long-term success depends on building sustainable competitive advantages:

Technology Differentiation

- Development of proprietary technologies and methodologies
- Creation of patent portfolios and IP protection
- Technology barriers to entry development

Network Effects

- Creation of multi-sided platforms whose value increases with user adoption
- Ecosystem lock-in through integrated services
- Development of community-driven growth mechanisms

Data Advantages

- Aggregation of unique data sets
- Development of proprietary algorithms and insights
- Creation of data network effects

Global Expansion Strategies

In today's interconnected world, startups must think globally from day one while executing effectively at the local level.

Cross-border Compliance Navigation

Regulatory Framework Management
- Jurisdiction-specific regulation knowledge
- Development of scalable compliance frameworks
- Creation of adaptive governance structures

Legal Strategy Development
- Appropriate structuring of corporate entities
- Intellectual property protection across jurisdictions
- Cross-border data flow management

Tax Optimization
- International tax implication knowledge
- Tax-efficient corporate structuring
- Compliance with transfer pricing regulations

Cultural Adaptation Frameworks

Market Entry Strategies
- Developing region-specific go-to-market approaches
- Adapting product offerings to suit local tastes
- Partnerships and network development at the local level

Team Development
- Diverse team training with cultural spectrums
- Cross-cultural management training
- Inclusive managerial competency building

Communication Protocols
- Clear lines of communication
- Localized marketing strategies
- Cultural adjustment principles

Integrating Sustainability

ESG considerations are no longer optional but integral to building a future-proof business.

Implementing ESG Metrics

Environmental Impact Management
- Computation of carbon footprint with reduction strategy
- Sustainable resource utilization plan
- Circular economy integration

Social Responsibility
- Stakeholder engagement programs
- Community impact initiatives
- Diversity and inclusion strategies

Governance Structures
- Transparent decision-making processes
- Ethical business practices
- Risk management frameworks

Impact Measurement Systems

Metric Development
- Definition of relevant impact metrics
- Description of measurement methodologies
- Implementation of tracking systems

Reporting Frameworks
- Creation of transparent reporting processes
- Integration into global standards
- Stakeholder communication strategies

Future-Proofing Strategies

Organizational Resilience

Building Resilient Organizations
- Development of flexible revenue streams
- Creation of crisis-resistant operations
- Implementation of agile decision-making processes

Team Development
- Creation of cross-functional capabilities
- Implementation of continuous learning programs
- Leadership pipeline development

Resource Management
- Efficient capital allocation strategies
- Development of sustainable supply chains
- Establishment of strategic partnerships

Innovation Management

R&D Strategy
- Balanced portfolio of incremental and disruptive innovation
- Development of strategic technology roadmap
- Management of research partnerships

Innovation Culture
- Encouraging experimentation
- Implementation of rapid prototyping processes

- Innovation metrics development

Key Suggestions to Entrepreneurs

To create truly future-proof startups, entrepreneurs should focus on:
1. **Strategic Agility**
    - Manage adaptable business models that evolve with the market
    - Create multiple scenarios for planning different future states
    - Embed redundancy in critical systems and processes
2. **Sustainable Growth**
    - Pay attention to unit economics early
    - Create scalable operations and systems
    - Integrate sustainable business practices
3. **Global Mindset**
    - Think globally, act locally
    - Build diversified, international teams
    - Develop cross-cultural competencies
4. **Technology Leadership**
    - Invest in core capability technology
    - Monitor emerging technologies
    - Build strong relationships with technology partners
5. **Stakeholder Management**
    - Engage all stakeholder groups
    - Build strong community relationships
    - Ensure transparent communication

Final Remarks

Building a future-proof startup in today's dynamic business environment requires a holistic approach that combines strategic positioning, global thinking, and sustainable practices. Success stems not just from initial innovation or market opportunity, but from building resilient organizations that can adapt to change while maintaining their core value proposition.

The most successful startups of the future will balance short-term market opportunities with long-term sustainability, technological innovation with human factors, and global reach with local relevance. Implementing the frameworks and strategies outlined in this chapter will help entrepreneurs build organizations that thrive, not just survive, in an increasingly complex and shifting business environment.

The journey of crafting a future-proof startup is continuous and evolving. It requires sustained monitoring of market changes, technological advances, and stakeholder needs, coupled with a clear vision and strong organizational culture. Only those who can navigate these challenges while staying true to their core mission will create lasting value in tomorrow's entrepreneurial ecosystem.

ACKNOWLEDGEMENT

In creating this book, I have been fortunate to draw upon the wisdom and expertise of an exceptional global network of partners and friends. Their contributions, both direct and indirect, have profoundly shaped this work, and I am deeply grateful for their influence. The following deserve special acknowledgements:

Kanth Krishnan, Managing Director at Accenture, whose visionary leadership and penetrating insights in technology services have been truly inspiring. His deep industry knowledge has substantially enriched this book's content.

Jeff Pappas, Managing Director at Newmark, who offered vital perspectives on the global real estate market landscape, bringing unmatched expertise to our exploration of diverse business environments.

Haitao Qi, Chairman of Devott Research and Advisory, whose illuminating insights on technology innovations and market trends, particularly in Asia, have been invaluable.

Charles Aird, former head of Outsourcing and Managed Services at PwC, whose comprehensive knowledge and strategic vision in outsourcing services have deeply informed my understanding of this crucial business function.

Mike Beares, Founder and Board Chairman of Clutch.co, whose entrepreneurial vision and commitment to connecting businesses with optimal service providers have significantly influenced my perspective on business connectivity.

Marc Schwarz, an industry pioneer in technology services, global sourcing, and innovation since the 1980s. His distinguished career spanning PwC, Deloitte, HP, and Sun Microsystems has yielded insights that have transformed our clients' businesses.

The merits of this book are a direct reflection of this exceptional global network, while any shortcomings are entirely my own responsibility.

Finally, I must express my deepest gratitude to my wife, Biyu, whose unwavering support and understanding have been fundamental to this endeavor. The intensive writing process, reminiscent of my doctoral dissertation at Yale twenty-five years ago, was made possible by her continuous encouragement. She remains the driving force behind both my professional growth and personal fulfillment.

ABOUT THE AUTHOR

Stephan S. Sunn

Stephan Sunn is the Executive Partner at Sanford Black Advisory, a preeminent global business and investment consultancy. In this capacity, he collaborates with industry leaders to advise companies worldwide on growth strategy, marketing/sales, innovation monetization, partnerships, and mergers & acquisitions. Over the past two decades, Mr. Sunn has consulted on sourcing provider selection for more than 30 international corporations and over 20 investment and M&A deals in the technology services, digital technologies, and global outsourcing sectors.

Mr. Sunn possesses particular expertise in empowering private enterprises to accelerate growth and enhance value creation through engagement with governments and technology parks. He holds a leadership position with Devott Co., China's largest private research firm focused on the IT, software, and technology services industries. Additionally, he serves as a Director at the China IT and Outsourcing Association. His clients span Fortune 500 companies, state-owned enterprises, technology parks, SMBs, and startups in both developed and emerging markets.

A graduate of the University of Science and Technology of China (USTC) with a Bachelor of Science degree, and Yale University with a Master of Science and Ph.D., Mr. Sunn frequently shares his insights and research as a speaker at global conferences and events. He is a prolific author and an accomplished presenter for his projects and clients around the world.

BOOKS BY THIS AUTHOR

Emerging Niche Industries
High-Growth Sectors Of The Future Jobs

The book "Emerging Niche Industries – High-Growth Sectors of Future Jobs" provides a roadmap for professionals seeking lucrative careers in specialized industries poised for significant expansion. It begins by highlighting the paradigm shift in career success, emphasizing adaptability, continuous learning, and the alignment of passion with prosperity as crucial to thriving in a dynamic job market. Traditional career paths are contrasted with niche careers, which allow for rapid growth, cross-border opportunities, and high earning potential in unique, underserved fields. Key areas of exploration include emerging technologies, such as artificial intelligence, cybersecurity, and biotechnology, which drive demand for highly specialized roles. The book also delves into the creative economy, where digital content creation and online education offer unprecedented monetization avenues, and sustainability sectors like renewable energy, food tech, and green building, which are critical in addressing global environmental challenges.

Additionally, the text addresses the financial sector's evolution through fintech, digital assets, and ESG investing, where professionals can shape sustainable investment trends. Niche opportunities in luxury markets and healthcare innovation also showcase high-reward roles for those with specialized skills and global perspectives.

For aspiring professionals, the book advocates for interdisciplinary skills, ethical considerations, and a global mindset as essential strategies for excelling in niche industries that balance wealth creation with meaningful, future-focused impact.

Asian Startup Failures: Lessons And Case Studies For Success

The book "Failures of Asian Startups: Key Lessons and Case Studies" examines the reasons for startup failures across Asia, emphasizing challenges stemming from internal dynamics, the broader Asian business environment, and country-specific factors. The book categorizes common failures into several themes, such as strategic misalignment, financial mismanagement, leadership struggles, and market entry challenges.

One prominent theme is the difficulty startups face in scaling operations due to Asia's diverse regulatory landscapes and fragmented markets, where cultural nuances and regulatory differences often hinder consistent growth. Many startups fail by adopting Western business models without adequate localization, leading to poor customer adoption and operational setbacks. Additionally, excessive reliance on venture capital for rapid scaling often pressures startups into unsustainable growth practices, such as high customer acquisition costs without a focus on retention, undermining long-term viability.

Through detailed case studies, including companies like Honestbee, Zilingo, and Ofo, the book underscores the importance of local adaptability, sustainable unit economics, and resilient operational models. It advocates for strategies like in-depth market research, localization, and balancing growth with profitability to foster sustainable success. By learning from these common pitfalls, the next generation of Asian entrepreneurs can build more resilient and culturally attuned businesses for the complex and dynamic Asian markets

Competing For The Growth: How Cities And Technology Parks Attract Global Trades And Investments

This book serves as a guidebook for city planners, economic development professionals, tech park builders, and public officials who aim to create thriving innovation communities that attract global trade and stimulate investments. It offers a structured path that begins with intangible factors like vision setting and partnership alignment and extends to pilots and full-blown magnet programs.

The book provides real-life instructions to help put these ideas into practice, including effective strategies for attracting rapidly growing businesses and talent, creating a setting that promotes innovation and entrepreneurship, fostering a competitive and appealing business climate, and building a globally recognized brand and reputation.

The author emphasizes that cities and tech parks must play to their strengths and assets to compete and win in the global arena. The race for relevance is on, and the window of opportunity to determine the outcome is closing. Cities and companies have what they need to succeed, and with the options, relationships, and guidance provided in this book, city managers and tech park authorities can make the decisions necessary to lead their communities to success in the world investment and trade arena.

Searching The New Profits: How The US SMEs And Startups Succeed In The Emerging Markets

In the face of global market turbulence and domestic uncertainties, American small and medium-sized businesses (SMBs) and startups have significant growth opportunities in emerging markets. However, these markets also present unique challenges. This handbook provides a semi-analytical and semi-prescriptive approach to help American SMBs and entrepreneurs succeed in these rapidly expanding markets. Conversely, governments, technology parks, and corporations in emerging countries can utilize this book to learn how to collaborate with U.S. companies in their markets to serve their customers effectively.

The book covers essential themes such as researching and identifying matching markets, choosing the appropriate market entry mode, local marketing and sales tactics, effective risk management, establishing an active and reputable presence in the local market, ensuring full legal compliance, avoiding political involvement, talent search and retention, and balancing standardization and localization. The final chapter shares valuable lessons from decades of business practices, acknowledging that readers may have different perspectives on these topics. Expanding knowledge through diverse viewpoints is beneficial for U.S. SMB and startup leaders. Despite the challenges, penetrating foreign markets can be highly profitable, and U.S. enterprises have a reasonable chance of success by capitalizing on the vast potential of these rapidly growing territories

Cracking The Winning Codes: How Global Vendors Win In The US Digital And Outsourcing Markets

This book serves as a comprehensive guide for international technology and outsourcing companies seeking to enter and succeed in the highly competitive U.S. market. It emphasizes the importance of adapting to the unique American business culture, which values innovation, diversity, relationships, customer-centricity, and results-oriented management. The guide highlights the need to navigate the complex U.S. regulatory landscape, including federal and state laws, as well as key legislations such as FCPA, SOX, and HIPAA.

The book covers essential topics such as understanding American business culture, complying with legal requirements, developing effective marketing strategies, employing successful sales techniques, addressing cultural differences, and managing risks associated with entering a new market. Additionally, it encourages the use of innovative tactics to differentiate from competitors and gain market share.

A special section titled "The Lessons" shares the author's personal experiences and insights, providing practical execution tips that focus on solution-oriented approaches, leveraging referrals and testimonials, managing communication costs, delivering higher quality than promised, and investing in proven local sales leaders.

By adhering to the core principles of understanding buyer preferences, continuous innovation, human capital development, risk management, customer-centricity, and resilient operations, global providers can successfully navigate and thrive in the lucrative U.S. market.

Win More Deals In The Digital Era: How Martech And Salestech Improve Marketing And Sales

In the new economy, businesses must navigate the complex landscape of Marketing Technology (Martech) and Sales Technology (Salestech) to stay competitive and drive growth. "Win More Deals in Digital Age" provides a comprehensive guide for leveraging these technologies to enhance customer experiences, streamline processes, and boost revenue across international markets.

The book explores the convergence of marketing, sales, and technology, emphasizing the importance of data-driven decision-making and cross-functional collaboration. It offers strategies for overcoming challenges in digital transformation, such as resistance to change and skills gaps, while also addressing the unique considerations of global expansion and localization. The authors predict future trends in Martech and Salestech, including the increasing role of AI, personalization, and emerging technologies like AR/VR and voice interfaces. Through real-world success stories from global brands like Coca-Cola, Sephora, and Airbnb, readers gain valuable insights into harnessing the power of these technologies for business success. This book serves as an essential resource for executives and professionals seeking to navigate the digital ecosystem and drive growth in the international marketplace

Renovations Or Revolutions: Impacts Of Latest AI On BPO And Contact Centers

The book "Renovation or Revolution? Impacts of Latest AI on BPO and Contact-centers Industries" provides an in-depth exploration of the transformative potential of artificial intelligence (AI) within the business process outsourcing (BPO) and contact center industries. It emphasizes the importance of early adoption, customization, and localization of AI solutions to gain a competitive edge in the global marketplace. The book highlights the evolving role of human agents, who will focus on complex problem-solving and relationship-building, while AI handles routine tasks. It also discusses the development of AI expertise within organizations and the ethical considerations surrounding AI implementation.

The authors present a roadmap for incorporating AI, underlining the need for a clear vision, employee training, and continuous improvement. Looking ahead, the book envisions a future of collaborative human-AI partnerships, hyper-personalization, and proactive customer engagement. It stresses that embracing AI is crucial for BPO and contact center companies to achieve sustainable growth and remain competitive in the international arena. The book serves as a comprehensive guide for executives navigating the AI revolution in the global business services industry.

Risky Reefs In The Ocean Of Global Markets: Common Mistakes Emerging Markets' Companies In Their Global Expansions

This book provides a comprehensive roadmap for emerging market companies venturing into global expansion. It highlights common pitfalls across strategic planning, finance, operations, human resources, marketing, technology, legal/ethics, and risk management. The book emphasizes thorough market research, cultural adaptation, local partnerships, brand building, innovation investment, and long-term vision.
As the global landscape evolves, it anticipates trends like digitization, sustainability integration, and talent acquisition challenges. The book provides corporate decision-makers with insights and best practices to navigate complexities, mitigate risks, and foster sustainable growth while driving innovation and progress internationally.

The AI Revolution In B2B Marketing And Sales: Disruptions Of AI In The Conventional B2B Markets

This professional guidance provides a comprehensive playbook for leveraging artificial intelligence (AI) to drive measurable results in B2B marketing and sales strategies. With insights from real-world case studies spanning diverse industries and business sizes, it explores AI's transformative impact on understanding the AI-empowered buyer, delivering personalized omnichannel experiences, boosting sales productivity, and optimizing operations.

The book offers a strategic framework for successful AI implementation, covering data readiness, talent acquisition, governance, and ethical considerations. Globally applicable principles foster human-AI collaboration, enabling organizations worldwide to harness AI's potential ethically and profitably in the B2B domain.

Promotor, Suppressor Or Neutralizer Impact Of Latest AI And Geopolitics On Global Outsourcing

This book explores how artificial intelligence (AI) and geopolitics are transforming the global outsourcing industry. It analyzes the strategic implications of AI for outsourcing operations, delivery models, talent management, and client relationships. The impact of geopolitical forces like trade tensions, political instability, and regulatory shifts on risk mitigation and geographic diversification is examined.

Emerging business models combining AI and human expertise, niche services, innovation through collaboration, workforce upskilling, and ethical AI governance are highlighted. The book provides a strategic roadmap for international outsourcing providers to navigate challenges, seize opportunities, and drive sustainable growth in this era of technological disruption and evolving geopolitical dynamics.

Pricing For Profitability And Growth: Mastering Pricing Strategies In Technology And Services Globally

This book explores how companies in the technology and service sectors can leverage strategic pricing to drive growth and profitability. It advocates moving beyond traditional cost-plus pricing to adopt value-based approaches that align pricing with customer perceptions of value. Key recommendations include: conducting thorough market research to understand customer needs and willingness to pay; segmenting customers and offering differentiated pricing tiers; leveraging data and analytics for dynamic pricing optimization; and aligning sales, marketing and pricing teams around a cohesive value proposition. The book emphasizes the importance of quantifying and communicating value to justify premium pricing.

Looking to the future, the book highlights how artificial intelligence and machine learning will transform pricing capabilities, enabling more personalized and responsive pricing strategies. It cautions against common pitfalls like failing to account for competitive responses or neglecting the psychology of pricing. Ultimately, the authors argue that pricing is a critical strategic capability that requires ongoing experimentation, cross-functional collaboration, and a willingness to adapt to changing market conditions. By taking a customer-centric, data-driven approach to pricing, technology and service companies can gain a powerful lever for sustainable growth and competitive advantage.

GovTech, Governance Technology: Unlocking Competitive Advantage For Cities And Tech Parks

This book dives into GovTech's potential to revolutionize government and urban development. By leveraging data, AI, and e-government platforms, GovTech can streamline processes, boost transparency, and even enhance citizen engagement. The book emphasizes collaboration between government, businesses, academia, and citizens to create a thriving GovTech ecosystem. Success stories from Estonia and Singapore showcase how GovTech can attract investment, streamline business operations, and fuel economic growth.

Furthermore, the book explores GovTech's role in fostering innovation hubs and simplifying business registrations, particularly for SMEs. It also delves into the power of data-driven governance and AI to transform public services and policymaking. Finally, the human aspect is crucial. Building a skilled workforce, managing cultural shifts, and promoting digital literacy are all emphasized for GovTech to reach its full potential.

www.ingramcontent.com/pod-product-compliance
Lightning Source LLC
Chambersburg PA
CBHW070110230526
45472CB00004B/1199